HOW TO HELP
A GUIDE TO
Giving
Back

WAYS TO HELP
CHILDREN
WITH DISABILITIES

Karen Bush
Gibson

Mitchell Lane
PUBLISHERS

P.O. Box 196
Hockessin, DE 19707
www.mitchelllane.com

Ways to Help After a Natural Disaster
Ways to Help Children With Disabilities
Ways to Help Chronically Ill Children
Ways to Help Disadvantaged Youth
Ways to Help in Your Community
Ways to Help the Elderly
Volunteering in Your School
Celebrities Giving Back

Copyright © 2011 by Mitchell Lane Publishers

All rights reserved. No part of this book may be reproduced without written permission from the publisher. Printed and bound in the United States of America.

PUBLISHER'S NOTE: The facts on which the story in this book is based have been thoroughly researched. Documentation of such research can be found on page 46. While every possible effort has been made to ensure accuracy, the publisher will not assume liability for damages caused by inaccuracies in the data, and makes no warranty on the accuracy of the information contained herein.

Library of Congress
Cataloging-in-Publication Data

Gibson, Karen Bush.
  Ways to help children with disabilities / by Karen Bush Gibson.
    p. cm.— (How to help: a guide to giving back)
  Includes bibliographical references and index.
  ISBN 978-1-58415-916-2 (library bound)
  1. Children with disabilities—Care. I. Title.
  HV888.G453 2010
  362.4083—dc22
                                2010006537

Printing   1   2   3   4   5   6   7   8   9

                                                PLB

CONTENTS

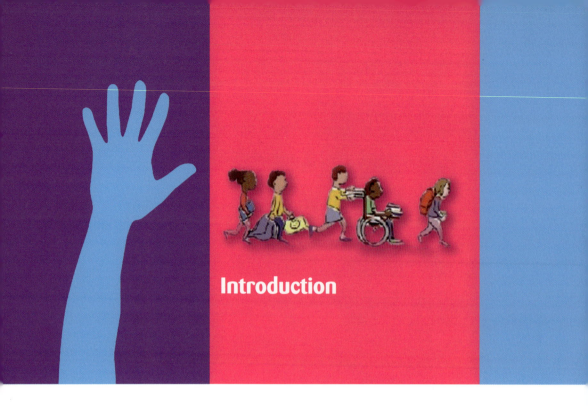

Introduction

When you see someone using a wheelchair, a Seeing Eye dog, or signing, you recognize that they have a disability. But do you understand what a disability is and its effect on a person?

A disability is an inability to perform an activity in what is considered a normal range. Physical and/or mental functioning is impaired in a way that causes a person's functioning to be restricted.

There are many words for disability, including *impairment* and *handicap*. Children with disabilities are also referred to as children with special needs, particularly in education. However, the word *disability* is currently used most often.

It's important to understand that when you put *disability* first in your language, such as *disabled person* or *special needs child,* you're putting the disability before the person or defining a person as disabled. A disability should never define an individual. Instead, you should put the person first in language, such as *a person with disabilities* or *a child with special needs.*

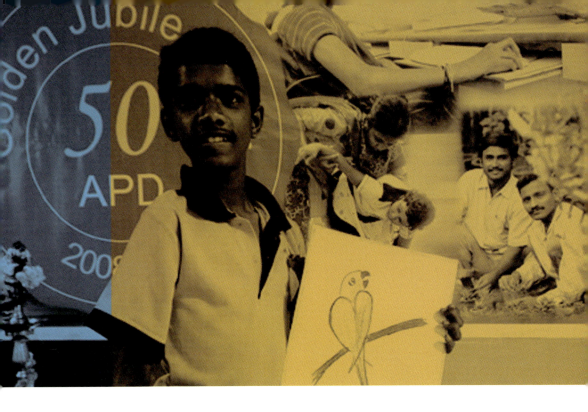

We can all use help at times. Children with disabilities are no different. Perhaps you know a child with a disability and want to help, but you don't know what to do. This book contains ideas for helping, from everyday interactions to more formal volunteer opportunities.

Helping a child with disabilities involves more than just desire. You must have the permission of a child's parents or guardians. You may need specialized training from a medical professional or a teacher. Talk over your interests with your parents and ask for their help in guiding you in the right direction for helping children with disabilities.

Guide dogs, also known as Seeing Eye dogs, can help children with visual and other disabilities safely move around.

What Is a Disability?

Learn more about disabilities that affect children.

Your parents can probably tell you how old you were when you crawled, walked, and talked. These are some of the many milestones that parents and pediatricians use to monitor a child's development.

Because everyone develops at a different rate, doctors and teachers often look at normal ranges of development. When a child isn't sitting up or making any type of noises by the age of one year old, they say the child has a developmental delay, because the child is developing more slowly than the normal range.

Experts have learned that early intervention can be very helpful to children who experience developmental delays. Most states and school systems have early intervention programs in which teachers, speech therapists, physical therapists, and occupational therapists work with children experiencing delays. Although many disabilities are chronic or lifelong, active treatment can help a child with a disability reach higher levels of functioning.

Some disabilities are physical, affecting a person's movement or physical functioning. Examples include paralysis, loss of a limb, blindness, or deafness. Physical disabilities can be the result of a disease or accident, or children may be born with a disability. An example is spina bifida, which means "open" or "split spine." Sometimes when a baby is in the womb, the spine or spinal cord doesn't grow the way it should. When this happens, the baby may be born with the spinal cord outside the bones of the spine. This happens to one in every one thousand babies born in the United States. Although the disabling effects of spina bifida vary according to where the opening is, most people with spina bifida suffer from some type of paralysis or loss of feeling below the waist that requires using braces or a wheelchair to get around.

Many organizations, such as United Cerebral Palsy and March of Dimes, have literature available for people to learn more about specific disabilities. You may see or hear the term *developmental disability*. Developmental disabilities are chronic conditions that begin in childhood but often last a lifetime. A developmental disability can affect physical and/or mental functioning and lead to challenges with daily activities, such as communicating, taking care of oneself, moving around, or learning.

The most common developmental disabilities are cerebral palsy, Down syndrome, and mental retardation. Some developmental disabilities occur from trauma at birth, such as cerebral palsy, which is caused by damage to a part of the brain that controls muscles. Other disabilities occur from an accident in which damage occurs to the brain or the brain goes too long without oxygen.

Down syndrome is one of many genetic conditions that are evident at birth. Another disabling condition that may be genetic but often isn't evident for the first two to three years of life is autism. People with autism most typically experience problems with social skills, communication, and behavior. According to the Centers for Disease Control and

Prevention, approximately one in every 150 children is diagnosed with autism or a related disability. A child with autism may offer no eye contact or not be interested in playing with others. Instead of speaking or pointing, a child with autism might lead you to what he or she wants. Repetitive behaviors such as rocking, spinning, or flapping fingers are common.

Not only are there a large number of types of disabilities, but each disability affects children in different degrees and ways. While it's important to know about specific disabilities that affect children you know and want to help, it is also important to know each child as an individual.

Children with disabilities are individuals first. Get to know them and their likes and dislikes.

When you meet with a child with a disability, just relax. Offer a smile or a simple greeting.

Chapter 2

Be Aware

Do not treat children with disabilities as if they were invisible.

Eva is a college graduate. She likes to write and take photographs. She also has cerebral palsy. Because cerebral palsy causes a lack of muscle control, Eva uses a motorized wheelchair to get around. In public, she uses a letter board for communicating with others. At home, she uses her computer. One of the ways she uses her computer is to blog about how she is treated as a person with a disability. She reports that many people treat her as if she were invisible or a small child.

When people don't have any experience with disabilities, they are often uncomfortable when faced with people who have them. Some people show this discomfort by ignoring individuals with disabilities.

Others may go to the other extreme of invading personal space and being too touchy. It's annoying for strangers to touch you and your things. It's also annoying to hear someone loudly making a big deal of you and the assistive devices that help you get around. Attention like this can be embarrassing for all concerned.

Never touch a guide dog without permission. The dog has been trained to do a job and needs to do it without distractions. If you're interested in guide dogs, you could join a puppy-raising club. The Seeing Eye organization partners with 4-H clubs in New Jersey, Pennsylvania, Delaware, Maryland, and New York to help foster families raise puppies until they're ready for training at about 16 to 18 months of age.

Approaching a Child with a Disability

When someone is different from you, do you know how they should be treated? The same way you would want to be treated. If someone is moving, whether with canes or a wheelchair, don't block their way by standing directly in front of them. Neither should you exaggerate moving out of their way. Treat any assistive devices used for mobility or being more independent as personal property. Motorized chairs may look cool, but they're a person's way of getting from one place to the next. A communication device is the person's way of speaking to others.

If an interaction involves more than a simple greeting, make it easier for the child. Looking up at someone from a wheelchair can strain muscles unnecessarily. Have a seat so that you can both be comfortable while you talk.

Speak to children with disabilities based on their age. Don't use baby talk with a child who is twelve. Would you like being talked to as if you were two years old? Although children with disabilities often have a parent or an aide present, speak directly to the child. If a person is communication impaired, ask yes or no questions at the beginning.

If an individual wants you to know why he is using a communication device or a wheelchair, he will tell you. And unless you're a medical professional with expertise in a specific disability, don't offer unsolicited advice. Never tell someone's business to other people. Remember to respect an individual's privacy just as you would want your privacy respected.

Visually impaired people are rarely hard of hearing, so there's no need to speak loudly or slowly. Just make certain that you identify yourself and warn them before you make any movements that may impact them. Visually impaired people in their own environment have everything in a specific place, so don't move things.

Many hearing-impaired people read lips, but this is hard to do when a person keeps moving her head. Stay still, but talk at a normal conversational pace. Touch a hearing-impaired person lightly on the arm to get her attention. Otherwise, respect personal space, no matter what the disability.

You're going to make mistakes. Everyone does. When you make a mistake in interactions with a child with a disability, apologize, learn from it, and move on.

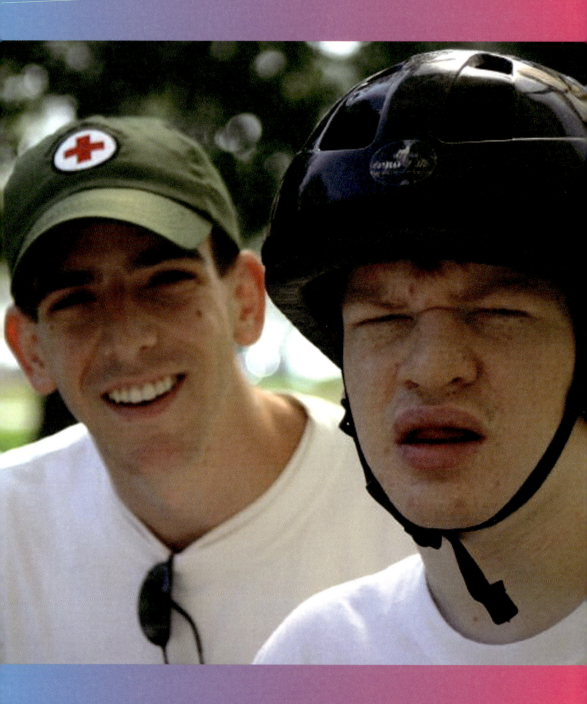

Volunteering at a camp for people with disabilities can be a great way to spend a summer.

Chapter 3

Be a Volunteer

Give your time to an organization that works with children who have disabilities.

An excellent way to help children with disabilities is through volunteering. Volunteering provides rewarding opportunities to help children. The challenge is to find the right match for your needs, skills, and interests. If you're a people person, you might be good with small groups or at fund-raising. A shy person might prefer working one on one with a child or helping with office work. Smaller organizations might be interested in your technological skills to get a web site up and running.

Don't let busy schedules keep you from volunteering. Most of us can spare an hour or two a week by turning off the television for that amount of time. Or consider working at a summer camp for children with disabilities. The National Dissemination Center for Children with Disabilities maintains a list of camp resources.

Where to Volunteer
Look at organizations within your community, such as hospitals and schools. Your local United Way office may know of a

group that works with children with disabilities. Talk with volunteer coordinators about what help is needed and what to expect. Remember to get permission from your parents.

Special Olympics is a worldwide athletic competition for people with disabilities. The program relies on large numbers of volunteers. They help with sports training, and they staff competitions. Most cities have a Ronald McDonald House near children's hospitals or university medical centers. Children with serious medical conditions have to make frequent trips to the hospital, and Ronald McDonald House provides a low-cost place for families to stay. When you help a family, you help the child as well.

What should you do if you can't find the right kind of volunteer work? Look for a need. In Bergen County, New Jersey, a group of people realized that the elderly and people with disabilities needed help with minor household repairs. They volunteered not only to make repairs, but also to install rails and smoke detectors for safety.

Training

Volunteers sometimes must learn new skills. Many organizations have training and orientation sessions. If training isn't available, ask to work with an experienced volunteer. At the beginning, you might do various tasks as you learn the ropes. Be open to new experiences, and remember that you're there to help an organization; it is not there to help you.

Service Learning

Schools throughout the United States are making volunteering a part of the curriculum through service learning projects with community organizations. The National Service-Learning Partnership reported that nearly 80,000 students, families, and teachers participated in the Third Annual Learn and Serve Challenge in 2009.

Talk to school officials about starting a service learning program in your school. Middle school students in Pennsylvania, for example, took what they learned about the importance of nutrition a step further by holding health fairs and operating a fresh fruit and vegetable stand in the community. You might come up with your own idea for volunteering with children with disabilities.

Have fun with volunteering! If you love what you do, you'll have a great time and perhaps encourage others to volunteer as well.

Many community organizations offer volunteer opportunities for young adults. Ask around to find a group that is a good fit for you. Even an hour or two of your time can make a difference.

Animals are often used as therapy for people with special needs. Just having a pet that needs you can make you feel special and help with stress. Pets are often looked at as "man's (or child's) best friends."

Everyday Helping

Help when there is a particular need.

There are going to be times when a child with a disability needs help. To pass by someone who needs help or who is experiencing an emergency is thoughtless. However, if you notice a child who you think might need help, ask first. It's very frustrating to have someone take over for you without asking if you need help. Often, an individual has the task in hand, but may need more time to complete it.

How does a person with a disability want to be treated? Like anyone else. A good rule of thumb is to put yourself in another person's place and ask how you would want to be treated.

Think about what kind of help you offer others in a day. If someone drops books or papers, you probably stop what you're doing and help them pick up their belongings. When someone's hands are full or busy, you might hold a door open for them. If you're on a bus or subway, or in a waiting area, it's polite to offer your seat to someone older than you. All of these things are everyday helpful things that you can do for anyone.

Watch for obstacles that make it difficult to get from one place to another. Push in chairs that block aisles. Pick up things that have been left on the floor, and be sure to wipe up spills. These things can make it dangerous to get from one place to another.

If a friend is having trouble with a task in science or art class, you would probably offer to help. Not take over, but just lend your assistance. What if someone in your class had difficulty with a task due to a disability? Couldn't you offer assistance in this situation too? Of course you could.

If you come upon a situation where you think an individual may need help, tactfully ask if you can offer assistance without making it a big deal. If the answer is yes, then listen

Sometimes the best way to help a child with a disability is to spend time together and do something fun. Playing games, listening to music, or going outdoors on a nice day are enjoyable ways to spend time.

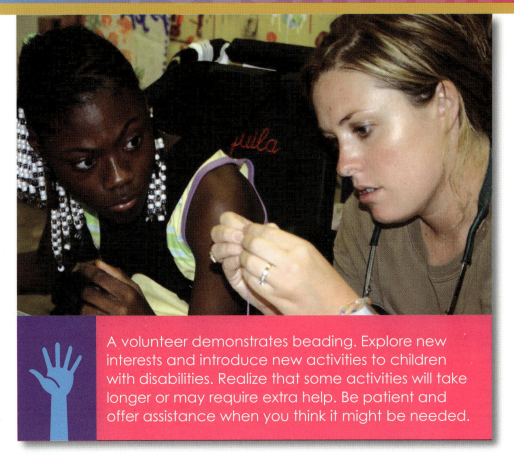

A volunteer demonstrates beading. Explore new interests and introduce new activities to children with disabilities. Realize that some activities will take longer or may require extra help. Be patient and offer assistance when you think it might be needed.

to any instructions—but allow an individual to decide whether or not she needs help.

Cues can give you a hint. For example, if a person is sitting or standing in front of a door, but is not moving, he or she may need help. If a person in a wheelchair is stopped, look to see if something is blocking his path.

Most of all, focus on the child, not on his or her disability. Children with disabilities are interested in lots of things—music, movies, television, sports, and more. Someone with a disability doesn't want your pity, just a normal interaction.

Ask a child with disabilities what his or her interests are. Most children enjoy some type of art and music. Many children also enjoy video games and sports.

The Many Ways to Communicate

Pay attention to the communication needs of a person.

Communication is a very powerful tool, yet not everyone can communicate with his or her voice. Some children with disabilities experience communication disorders. Some disorders, such as cerebral palsy, can affect the muscle control needed to form words. When this happens, augmentative or alternative communication is needed. A basic augmentative tool is a picture board. Common requests are illustrated with photos. A person with a disability might choose a picture by pointing, looking, or aiming a light pointer at it.

With constant advances in technology, the development of electronic communication devices for children with disabilities is very exciting. For example, LightWRITER™ Text-to-Speech communication devices allow users to type what they want to say, and this is transmitted in voice output.

Computer adaptations have made the world more accessible for many children. Children who experience problems with motor skills can still log on to chat rooms on the Internet, send e-mails, or write letters through voice commands or touch screens. A company called Tobii

Technology manufactures a tablet PC called MyTobiiP10. Instead of receiving commands through a traditional keyboard, it uses eye-tracking software.

Telephones can also be adapted as teletypewriters (TTY) or telecommunications devices for the deaf (TDD). TTY or TDD units can be used even if only one telephone is attached. Dialing 711 connects you to a telephone relay operator with the telephone company, who will send a text to a TTY unit.

Other children with special needs, particularly those who move independently, might prefer to communicate using American Sign Language (ASL), as electronic devices can be difficult to carry around. ASL courses are easy to find. As with any new language, proficiency comes with use.

Communication Tips

Not everyone has access to communication devices, which can be very expensive and hard to use for people with some disabilities. Many people rely on existing verbal skills, yet it can be very frustrating for the speaker who can't make himself understood. Here are some tips on communicating with a child who has a communication disability:

- Don't pretend to understand what someone says when you don't. Apologize and ask for it to be repeated.
- Repeat what you think you heard if you're not sure.
- Some people experience problems processing or understanding communication that they hear. Be patient and take whatever time is needed.
- Ask questions that can be answered with a nod or shake of the head when communication is difficult.
- Always look at the person you're speaking with, not another person who may be interpreting.

- Allow individuals to finish their own sentences.
- Speak naturally to people with speech impairments.

Spend time communicating with children who have disabilities, and learn about alternative communication. Finding a way to communicate makes all the difference for a child who is challenged by communication disabilities.

Augmentative communication devices allow children with communication disabilities to communicate with others. These devices can range from sign boards to electronic devices.

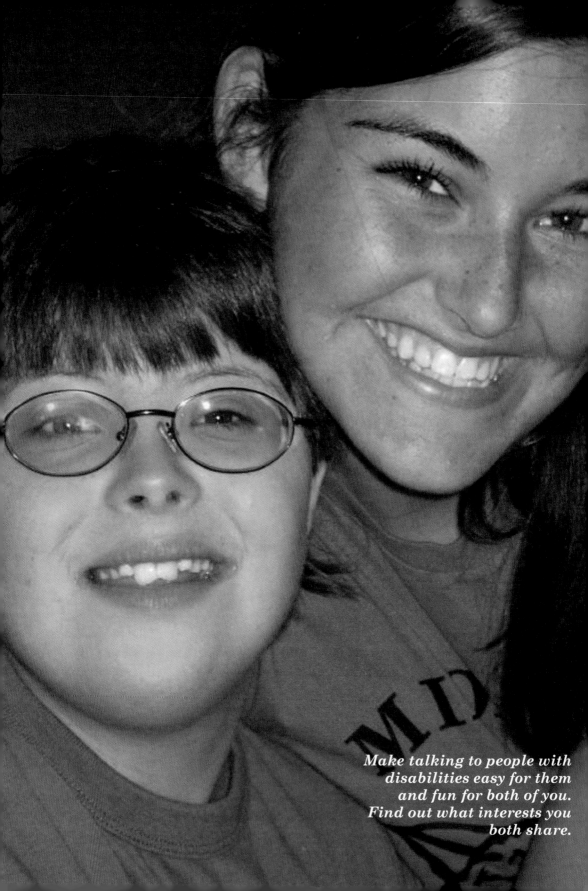

Make talking to people with disabilities easy for them and fun for both of you. Find out what interests you both share.

Chapter **6**

Look Beyond Behavioral Problems

Life can be tough, particularly if a disability keeps a child from doing or saying what he or she wants.

Tackling life with a disability is a challenge. Things that come easily to many people may not come easily to a child with a disability. Occasionally, frustration leads to bad behavior.

Having a disability isn't an excuse for acting out, but that doesn't mean you can't learn from a situation. If someone insists on helping you even when you tell that person that you don't need help, that might explain a tantrum, particularly if the same thing happens day after day. Tears of frustration can come from being extremely thirsty, yet unable to get a drink of water to your mouth. What if you're asking for help to get to the bathroom, but no one understands what you're saying? Or perhaps you want to get inside a building, but the only way in has steps and you're in a wheelchair? Any of these situations can lead to a behavioral meltdown.

Look for cues or triggers that may set off an outburst of poor behavior. For example, behavioral problems are frequently tied to communication problems. Try to look at a situation or the environment from the eyes of the child.

Sometimes, simple adjustments can make the difference between tears and smiling faces.

Learning Disability

Children who suffer from ongoing behavioral problems may have an undiagnosed learning disability. An untreated learning disability creates feelings of failure and frustration, which can lead to acting out. Be aware of inconsistencies in behavior, such as a child who can recite complex details from last night's television program, but who can't remember a teacher's instructions from five minutes ago. Share any observations between a task or the environment and acting out with a teacher or therapist.

Sometimes the disability that a child suffers from goes hand in hand with poor behavior. Emotional behavioral disability (EBD), for example, is a condition of extreme and chronic behavior that is outside the norms of what society deems acceptable and appropriate. When a child has a primary diagnosis of EBD, treatment includes a consistent behavior plan that everyone needs to know.

Responding to Poor Behavior

While life can be frustrating for a child with a disability, it is never acceptable to be verbally or physically abusive to others. Make certain a child understands acceptable behavior by modeling it yourself.

When an episode of poor behavior ends, review what happened and see if you can find the trigger to the behavior. Talk the situation over with a supervisor or experienced volunteer to gain insight into specific responses.

Independence

All of us want to be independent. Even the smallest child will exclaim, "Me do it!" A child with a disability wants to be independent like you. Give a child with special needs the tools and time to complete a task, and you might see behavioral problems vanish.

Special Olympics allows people with disabilities to demonstrate their independence and winning spirit. This organization services over 3 million athletes in more than 150 countries.

Chapter 7

Understand the Differences Between Mental and Physical Disabilities

Never make assumptions. Get to know a child and how a disability affects his or her life.

Physical or communication challenges don't necessarily affect intelligence. Someone can be confined to a wheelchair or not able to communicate verbally, but still be every bit as smart as or smarter than you. Think of the physicist Stephen Hawking, who has motor neurone disease but is a genius. Likewise, someone who is mentally challenged may be physically very capable.

Unfortunately, people make assumptions all the time. A common assumption is that someone who has cerebral palsy or any of the other conditions that affect speech muscles also experiences mental retardation. Although sometimes the two do occur together, it should never be assumed. Many people with physical disabilities attend college and reach professional success. The inability to speak verbally is not tied to intelligence.

Neither is intelligence related to the use of a wheelchair, canes, or even an awkward gait. Issues with mobility only tell the observer that special physical challenges exist.

Cognitive Disabilities

People with cognitive disabilities such as mental retardation may have unique facial characteristics, but other people with cognitive impairments present a normal appearance. A diagnosis of mental retardation must meet several criteria. The disability occurs before age 18, an IQ score is 70 or below, and functional limitations occur. Sometimes the cause isn't known, but cognitive disabilities can be related to heredity, early environment, or injury to the brain. Among people with mental retardation, there are various levels of functioning, from high functioning to profound retardation.

Children with mental retardation are eligible for educational services through the public school system until the age of 21. Any child with special needs related to a disability is provided with an individualized education program (IEP), which details a child's educational placement, support services, adaptations, and a plan for the school year. Whenever possible, children with special needs are served in the general classroom with modifications, such as an aide.

As a child with cognitive deficits reaches the secondary school level, the IEP or curriculum may include lessons in functional life skills, such as cooking, and job skills.

Helping a Child With Severe Deficits

When children with severe disabilities face significant physical and mental challenges, living independently is not a choice. These children will likely live with family or in a residential living situation for their entire lives. Both families and residential programs use volunteers to help with activities of daily living, such as feeding and dressing.

Because caring for someone with severe disabilities is a 24-hour-a-day situation, families benefit from occasional respite care. Respite provides temporary care to individuals with disabilities while caregivers take a break to care for themselves or other family members.

Chapter 8

Learn What Interests a Child Has

Sometimes the best way to help a child with a disability is to encourage special interests.

What do you like to do when you're not in school? Reading, playing video games, listening to or playing music, drawing, participating in or watching sports, using the computer, and spending time with pets are just some of the interests or hobbies that young people enjoy, regardless of abilities.

Experts have found that our quality of life improves when we participate in interests outside of work (or school). While you can gain special skills or knowledge with many hobbies, ultimately it is the sense of fulfillment that makes hobbies worth pursuing.

Children with disabilities have special interests that have nothing to do with their disability. Perhaps a child is a fan of the Harry Potter or Twilight series of books. If so, share that interest by reading the books, watching the movies, or exploring fan sites together.

Following professional sports is another interest you could share, even if one of you is a Red Sox fan and the other is a Yankees fan. Video games are fun to play, and game systems such as the Nintendo® Wii make adapting video games to abilities that much easier.

Discovering Special Interests

The easiest way to find out what a child with special needs is interested in is to simply ask. If for some reason that doesn't work (sometimes we don't realize what we like or are shy about sharing), consider asking a family member. Again, look for clues. A child who wears classic rock T-shirts may enjoy music from the '60s, '70s, or '80s. If a child smiles when he or she sees a dog, cat, or horse, perhaps you're with an animal lover. Specific programs combining individuals with disabilities with dogs or horses have been quite successful. "Saddle Up!" is a program in Tennessee that provides therapeutic horse riding to children with disabilities. Other therapeutic riding programs can be found through the American Entertainment and Equestrian Alliance.

Explore the Sensory World

If a child truly doesn't seem to have any special interests, perhaps you can introduce the child to new activities. Activities involving touch can be beneficial to those who experience certain impairments. Always check with a caregiver or supervisor before trying a new activity with a child. Some children experience an aversion to some textures.

How about gardening? Digging in the dirt not only feels good, but a child gets the added benefit of watching something grow. Art is another activity with sensory benefits. Use big pieces of butcher paper and various mediums, from crayons to finger paint, for free expression.

A child with a disability is more than the disability. He or she will appreciate spending time doing favorite activities and learning new things.

Another way to help children with disabilities is by participating in fund-raisers. These could include a garage sale, bake sale, or even more inventive ideas.

Chapter 9

Make It Happen Through Fund-raising

Put your energy and creativity to work by participating in fund-raising activities.

Organizations that work with children with disabilities have expenses, from the cost of maintaining an office to buying items that directly benefit the children. Fund-raising can help them, and it can also aid research.

Some organizations use volunteers in annual fund-raisers—for answering the phones during a muscular dystrophy telethon, picking up donations for the United Way, or collecting pledges for a walk-a-thon. Other charities operate on such a small scale that they don't have the manpower for fund-raising. This is where you can help. All you need is a little creativity in thinking up fund-raising ideas. Let your imagination take you beyond selling cookie dough, candy bars, and car washes.

Perhaps you and some friends can advertise a monthly parents' night out, where you provide pizza, games, and baby-sitting for a low cost. Older children might enjoy a regular board game night. Borrow board games that don't take too long to play (no Monopoly!) and charge a dollar to play each game. Hold tournaments, with game winners advancing to the next level of play. Award a grand prize of a small gift or gift certificate. You can also hold a video game tournament as long as you have access to multiple game consoles, TVs, and video game copies. Make certain that people know who will benefit from the money you're raising; you may earn extra in tips from parents.

Enlist Schools or Businesses

A Kansas junior high school raised $3,251.85, much of it in pennies, for a local charity. Why so much? Kids donated money for the opportunity to throw a pie at some good-natured teachers and even the school superintendent. A penny isn't very much, but when you put thousands of them together, they can add up to quite a bit. Choose a child with disabilities whose family is struggling with the cost of care and treatment. With the family's permission and school support, hold a "pennies for [that family]" week in which everyone brings in their pennies.

Does your school have a rule about not wearing hats? If so, ask the principal to hold a hat day where everyone who brings a dollar can wear a hat for a day. Perhaps you and some friends can take over concessions for some home games, with proceeds going to a child with a disability or an organization that works with people with disabilities.

Check with businesses in your community about donations for a raffle. Businesses can also support school carnivals with donations and prizes. You can provide those businesses with free publicity in programs and on school marquees.

Make Some Noise!

Fund-raising is much more successful when people know about it. Contact your community newspaper about your efforts and where the money will be going. If your community is large enough, contact radio and television stations as well. A well-placed newspaper article or spot on the local news does wonders for spreading the word.

Why not hold a carnival at your school? The proceeds could benefit the family of a child with disabilities, or an organization that helps children with disabilities.

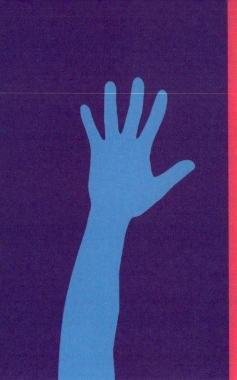

Chapter 10

Be a Friend

Look beyond the disability. Just as you are more than the color of your hair or your height, so is a child with a disability.

What is a friend? A friend is someone who:

- supports you
- spends time with you
- makes you smile
- accepts you as you are
- is trustworthy

In a 2006 study, the Center for Educational Networking found that children with disabilities listed physical play, friends, and pets as most important for their quality of life. Yet forming friendships can be challenging for children with disabilities. Children with disabilities tend to be more isolated than others, as many of their peers do not understand disabilities. While many people wouldn't think of laughing at or making fun of someone who is of a different race, people with disabilities don't always receive the same type of consideration. Social isolation can lead to depression. All of these obstacles can affect a child's progress.

Children should be involved in social activities, because, according to the University of Michigan, those who develop good social skills in elementary school often have better academic skills and better relationships as adults. Younger children might need parents to set up play dates, while it's more effective to plan group outings, such as scouting or church youth groups, for older children.

Buddy systems or peer teaching programs in schools regularly expose children with disabilities to others in their age group. Friendships with people in other age groups are also valuable. Model characteristics that are valued in friendships, such as sharing and problem-solving skills.

Advocate for Children with Disabilities

Another thing that friends and concerned people do is advocate for each other. To advocate is to educate and show your support. By speaking out, you bring a subject or issue to the public's attention. Sometimes a disability makes advocating for oneself a challenge. Children with disabilities deserve advocates to speak on their behalf about basic human rights, legal rights, and rights in education and medical care.

Know what rights individuals with disabilities have. Become familiar with the Americans with Disabilities Act (ADA), which became effective in 1990. The ADA addresses discrimination, accessibility to public buildings, transportation, accommodations, employee rights, availability of telecommunications devices and services for the hearing and speech impaired, and guidelines for resolving disputes.

If you are successful advocating for children with special needs, help them learn how to advocate for themselves as they grow older. Be a friend, and help children with disabilities live a more enjoyable life.

RESOURCES

National Organizations with Local Offices

AbilityHub—Assistive Technology Solutions
c/o The Gilman Group, L.L.C.
P.O. Box 6356
Rutland, VT 05702-6356
http://www.abilityhub.com/

American Association of People
 with Disabilities (AAPD)
1629 K Street NW, Suite 950
Washington, DC 20006
Phone: (800) 840-8844 (Toll Free V/TTY)
http://aapd-dc.org/

Autism Society
4340 East West Hwy, Suite 350
Bethesda, Maryland 20814
http://www.autism-society.org/

Council for Exceptional Children (CEC)
1110 North Glebe Rd., Suite 300
Arlington, VA 22201
Phone: (888) 232-7733
http://www.cec.sped.org/

National Dissemination Center for Children with
 Disabilities (NICHCY)
1825 Connecticut Ave NW, Suite 700
Washington, DC 20009
Phone: 800-695-0285 (Voice/TTY)
Phone: 202-884-8200 (Voice/TTY)
http://www.nichcy.org/

Special Olympics International
1325 G St. NW, Suite 500
Washington, DC 20005
Phone: (202) 628-3630
http://www.specialolympics.org/

Through the Looking Glass
2198 Sixth Street, Suite 100
Berkeley, CA 94710-2204
Phone: (800) 644-2666 (VOICE)
TTY: (510) 848-1005
http://lookingglass.org/

United Cerebral Palsy (UCP) National
1660 L Street, NW, Suite 700
Washington, DC 20036
Phone: (800) 872-5827
http://www.ucp.org/

Alabama

Alabama Council for Developmental Disabilities
100 North Union Street
P.O. Box 301410
Montgomery, AL 36130-1410
Phone: (800) 232-2158
http://www.acdd.org/

Alabama Disabilities Action Coalition
206 13th Street South
Birmingham, AL 35233-1317
http://accessalabama.org/

Alaska

Association for the Education of Young Children
Southeast Alaska
PO Box 22870
Juneau, AK 99802-2870
Phone: (888) 785-1235
http://www.aeyc-sea.org/

Thread Alaska
3350 Commercial Drive, Suite 203
Anchorage, AK 99501
Phone: (800) 278-3723
http://www.threadalaska.org/

Arizona

Arizona Department of Health Services
150 North 18th Avenue
Phoenix, AZ 85007
Phone: (602) 542-1025
http://www.azdhs.gov/division.htm/

Upward Foundation
6306 North 7th Street
Phoenix, AZ 85014
Phone: (602) 279-5801
http://www.upwardfoundation.org/

Arkansas

Disability Rights Center, Inc.
1100 North University, Suite 201
Little Rock, AR 72207
Phone: (800) 482-1174 V/TTY
http://www.arkdisabilityrights.org/

Easter Seals Arkansas Children's Rehabilitation
3918 Woodland Heights Road
Little Rock, AR 72212
Phone: (501) 219-4000
http://ar.easterseals.com/

California

State Council on Developmental Disabilities
1507 21st Street, Suite 210
Sacramento, CA 95811
Phone: (866) 802-0514
http://www.scdd.ca.gov/

Support for Families of Children with Disabilities
2601 Mission Street, Suite 606
San Francisco, CA 94110
Phone: (415) 282-7494
http://www.supportforfamilies.org/

Tuolumne Trails
22988 Ferretti Road
Groveland, CA 95321
Phone: (800) 678-5102
http://www.tuolumnetrails.org/

Colorado

Colorado Developmental Disabilities Council
3401 Quebec Street, Suite 6009
Denver, CO 80207
Phone: (720) 941-0176
http://www.coddc.org/

PEAK Parent Center in Colorado Springs
611 North Weber, Suite 200
Colorado Springs, CO 80903
Phone: (719) 531-9400
http://www.peakparent.org

Connecticut
Connecticut Council on Developmental
  Disabilities
460 Capitol Avenue
Hartford, CT 06106-1308
Phone: (800) 653-1134
http://www.ct.gov/ctcdd/

The Learning Disabilities Association of
  Connecticut, Inc.
999 Asylum Avenue, 5th Floor
Hartford, CT 06105
Phone: (860) 560-1711
http://www.ldact.org/

Delaware
Delaware Developmental Disabilities Council
M. O'Neill Building
410 Federal St.
Dover, DE 19901
Phone: (302) 739-2232
http://ddc.delaware.gov/

Delaware Foundation Reaching Citizens
640 Plaza Drive
Four Seasons Center
Newark, DE 19702
Phone: (302) 454-2730
http://www.dfrcfoundation.org/

Florida
Camp I-Am-Special
235 Marywood Drive
St. Johns, FL 32259
Phone: (904) 230-7447
http://www.dosacamps.com/

The Special Needs Color Guard of America
c/o The Florida Special Arts Center, Inc.
10258 NW 46th Street
Sunrise, FL 33351
Phone: (954) 721-1020
http://www.flsac.org/

Georgia
ATL3, Inc.—Assistive Technology & Learning Co.
2524 Flair Knoll Drive N.E.
Atlanta, GA 30345
Phone: (404) 697-3182
http://www.at4learning.com/

Beyond Words Center Summer Program
1762 Century Boulevard, NE, Suite B
Atlanta, GA 30345
Phone: (404) 633-0250
http://www.beyondwordscenter.com/

Hawaii
Kapi'olani Deaf Center and
  Gallaudet University Regional Center
4303 Diamond Head Road
Manono Building #102
Honolulu, HI 96816
Phone: (808) 734-9210 (V/TTY)
http://www.kcc.hawaii.edu/object/kdc.html

Programs for People with Developmental
  Disabilities
Developmental Disabilities Division
Hawaii State Department of Health
1250 Punchbowl, #463
P. O. Box 3378
Honolulu, HI 96801
Phone: (808) 586-5842
http://hawaii.gov/health/disability-services/
  developmental/index.html

Idaho
Center on Disabilities and Human Development
University of Idaho
121 West Sweet Avenue
Moscow, Idaho 83843
Phone: (800) 393-7290
http://www.idahocdhd.org/dnn/

Summit Assistance Dogs
7575 Chestnut Lane
Anacortes, WA 98221
Phone: (360) 293-5609
http://www.summitdogs.org/

Illinois
Autism Society of America
Central Illinois Chapter
P.O. Box 8781
Springfield, IL 62791-8781
Phone: (217) 241-2023
http://www.asacic.org/

Brain Injury Association of Illinois
P.O. Box 64420
Chicago, IL 60664-0420
Phone: (800) 699-6443
http://www.biail.org/

Indiana
Indiana Down Syndrome Foundation
3050 N. Meridian Street
Indianapolis, IN 46208
Phone: (888) 989-9255
http://www.indianadsf.org/

VSA Arts of Indiana
Harrison Centre for the Arts
1505 N. Delaware Street
Indianapolis, IN 46202
Phone: (317) 974-4123
http://www.vsai.org/

Iowa
Camp Courageous
12007 190th Street
Monticello, IA 52310-0418
Phone: (319) 465-5916
http://www.campcourageous.org/

Iowa Compass: Information and Referral
    Center for Disabilities and Development
The University of Iowa
100 Hawkins Drive #295
Iowa City, IA 52242-1011
Phone: (800) 779-2001
http://www.iowacompass.org/

Kansas
Kansas Federation of the Council for Exceptional
    Children
1920 N. 66th
Kansas City, KS 66102
Phone: (913) 288-4080
http://www.kansascec.org/

TARC
2701 S.W. Randolph
Topeka, KS 66611
Phone: (785) 232-0597
http://www.tarcinc.org/

Kentucky
Kentucky Disabilities Coalition
P.O. Box 1589
Frankfort, KY 40602
Phone (800) 977-7505
http://www.geocities.com/kydisabilitiescoalition

Kentucky Education Rights Center, Inc.
1323 Moores Mill Road
Midway, KY 40347
Phone: (859) 983-9222
http://www.edrights.com/

Louisiana
Louisiana Citizens for Action Now (LACAN)
2313 Blue Haven Drive
New Iberia, LA 70563
Phone: (337) 367-7407
http://www.lacanadvocates.org/

Louisiana Health and Rehabilitation Center, Inc.
1033 N. Lobdell Avenue
Baton Rouge, LA 70806
Phone: (225) 231-2490
http://www.lahealthandrehab.org/

Maine
Maine Center on Deafness (MCD)
68 Bishop Street, Suite 3
Portland, ME 04103
Phone: (800) 639-3884 (V/TTY)
http://www.mcdmaine.org/

Pine Tree Society
149 Front Street
Bath, ME 04530
Phone: (207) 443-3341
http://www.pinetreesociety.org/

Maryland
Family Net Works Program
217 E. Redwood Street, Suite 1300
Baltimore, MD 21202
Phone: (301) 642-2277
http://www.family-networks.org/

Maryland School for the Blind
3501 Taylor Avenue
Baltimore, MD 21236
Phone: (410) 444-5000
http://www.mdschblind.org/

Massachusetts
Greater Boston Arc
221 N. Beacon Street, 2nd Floor
Boston, MA 02135
Phone: (617) 783-3900, ext. 20
http://www.arcgb.org/

New England INDEX
Shriver Center UMASS Medical School
200 Trapelo Road
Waltham, MA 02452-6319
Phone: (800) 642-0249
http://www.disabilityinfo.org/

Michigan
Greater Detroit Agency for the Blind and Visually
    Impaired
16625 Grand River Avenue
Detroit, MI 48227
Phone: (313) 272-3900
http://www.gdabvi.org/

University Center for the Development of
    Language and Literacy
University of Michigan
1111 E. Catherine Street
Ann Arbor, MI 48109-2054
Phone: (734) 764-8440
http://www.languageexperts.org/

Minnesota
Courage Center
3915 Golden Valley Road
Minneapolis, MN 55422
Phone: (763) 588-0811
http://www.courage.org/

Minnesota State Council on Disability
121 E. 7th Place, Suite 107
St. Paul, MN 55101
Phone: (800) 945-8913 (V/TTY)
http://www.disability.state.mn.us

Mississippi
EMPOWER Community Resource Center
P.O. Box 1733
136 S. Poplar Street
Greenville, MS 38702-1733
Phone: (800) 337-4852
http://www.msempower.org/

Missouri
Missouri Planning Council for
  Developmental Disabilities
1706 E. Elm
P.O. Box 687
Jefferson City, MO 65102
Phone: (800) 500-7878
http://www.mpcdd.com/

Rehabilitation Services for the Blind
Family Support Division
615 Howerton Court
P.O. Box 2320
Jefferson City, MO 65102-2320
Phone: (800) 592-6004
http://www.dss.mo.gov/fsd/rsb/

Montana
Montana Access to Outdoor Recreation (MATOR)
634 Eddy Avenue, CHC-009
Missoula, MT 59812
Phone: (406) 243-5751
(877) 243-5511 (toll-free in-state only)
http://recreation.ruralinstitute.umt.edu/Mator/
  index.asp

Support & Techniques for Empowering People
  (S.T.E.P.) Inc.
1501 14th Street West, Suite 210
Billings, MT 59102
Phone: (888) 866-3822 (V/TTY)
http://www.msubillings.edu/mtcd

Nebraska
The Arc of Nebraska
1672 Van Dorn Street
Lincoln, NE 68502
Phone: (402) 475-4407
http://www.arc-nebraska.org/

People First of Nebraska
345 S. G Street
Broken Bow, NE 68822
Phone: (308) 872-6490
http://www.peoplefirstofnebraska.org/

Nevada
Nevada Disability Advocacy and Law Center
6039 Eldora Avenue, Suite C, Box 3
Las Vegas, NV 89146
Phone: (888) 349-3843 (toll-free)
http://www.ndalc.org/

University Center for Excellence in
  Developmental Disabilities
Research and Education Planning Center
College of Education/MS285
University of Nevada-Reno
Reno, NV 89557
Phone: (800) 216-7988
http://repc.unr.edu/

New Hampshire
National Spinal Cord Injury Association
54 Wentworth Avenue
Londonderry, NH 03053
Phone: (603) 479-0560
http://www.nhspinal.org/

New Hampshire Family Voices
93 Pleasant Street
Concord, NH 03301
Phone: (800) 852-3345, ext. 4525
http://www.nhfv.org/

New Jersey
Alliance for the Betterment of Citizens with
  Disabilities
127 Route 206, Suite 18
Hamilton, NJ 08610
Phone: (609) 581-8375
http://www.abcdnj.org/

The Seeing Eye Inc.
10 Washington Valley Rd.
P.O. Box 375
Morristown, NJ 07963
Phone: (973) 539-4425
http://www.seeingeye.org/

New Mexico
New Mexico State Library for the Blind and
  Physically Handicapped
1209 Camino Carlos Rey
Santa Fe, NM 87507-5166
Phone: (800) 456-5515
http://www.nmstatelibrary.org/

New Mexico Technology Assistance Program
435 St. Michael's Drive, Building D
Santa Fe, NM 87505
Phone: (800) 659-1779 (V)
http://www.nmtap.com/

New York
Family Empowerment Council, Inc.
225 Dolson Avenue, Suite 403
Middletown, NY 10940
Phone: (845) 343-8100
http://www.familyempowerment.org/

United We Stand of New York
91 Harrison Avenue
Brooklyn, NY 11206
Phone: (718) 302-4313
http://www.uwsofny.org/

North Carolina
North Carolina Council on Developmental
  Disabilities
3801 Lake Boone Trail, Suite 250
Raleigh, NC 27607
Phone: (800) 357-6916
http://www.nccdd.org/

Recording for the Blind & Dyslexic (RFB&D)
25 Birnham Lane
Durham, NC 27707
Phone: (919) 599-4104
http://www.rfbd.org/

North Dakota
North Dakota School for the Deaf
1401 College Drive North
Devils Lake, ND 58301
Phone: (877) 630-6214
http://www.nd.gov/ndsd/

North Dakota Vision Services
500 Stanford Road
Grand Forks, ND 58203
Phone: (800) 421-1181
http://www.ndvisionservices.com/

Ohio
Easter Seals Central and Southeast Ohio
565 Children's Drive West
P.O. Box 7166
Columbus, OH 43205
Phone: (614) 228-5523
http://www.eastersealscentralohio.org

Ohio Family and Children First
30 E. Broad Street, 8th Floor
Columbus, OH 43215
Phone: (614) 752-4044
http://www.ohiofcf.org/

Oklahoma
J.D. McCarty Center for Children with
  Developmental Disabilities
2002 E. Robinson Street
Norman, OK 73071
Phone: (405) 307-2800
http://www.jdmc.org/

Oklahoma Office of Disability Concerns
2401 N.W. 23rd, Suite 90
Oklahoma City, OK 73107
Phone: (800) 522-8224
http://www.odc.ok.gov/

Oregon
The Arc of Oregon
1745 State Street
Salem, OR 97301
Phone: (877) 581-2726
http://www.arcoregon.org/

Oregon Brain Injury Resource Network
345 N. Monmouth Avenue
Monmouth, OR 97361
Phone: (877) 872-7246
http://www.tr.wou.edu/tbi

Pennsylvania
National Federation of the Blind of Pennsylvania
42 S. 15th Street, Suite 222
Philadelphia, PA 19102
Phone: (215) 988-0888
http://www.nfbp.org/

Pennsylvania Parents and Caregivers Resource
  Network
P.O. Box 4336
Harrisburg, PA 17111-0336
Phone: (888) 572-7368
http://www.ppcrn.org/

Rhode Island
Advocates in Action
P.O. Box 41528
Providence, RI 02940-1528
Phone: (800) 745-5555
http://www.aina-ri.org/

VSA Arts of Rhode Island
500 Prospect Street
Pawtucket, RI 02860
Phone: (401) 725-0247
http://www.vsartsri.org/

South Carolina
Disability Action Center, Inc.
1115 Belleview Street
Columbia, SC 29201
Phone: (803) 779-5121
http://www.dacsc.org/

Family Connection of South Carolina, Inc.
2712 Middleburg Drive, Suite 103-B
Columbia, SC 29204
Phone: (800) 578-8750
http://www.familyconnectionsc.org/

South Dakota
South Dakota Cares
1351 N. Harrison Avenue
Pierre, SD 57501
Phone: (800) 592-1852
http://www.southdakotacares.org/

South Dakota Coalition of Citizens with Disabilities
221 South Central Avenue
Pierre, SD 57501
Phone: (800) 210-0143
http://www.sd-ccd.org/

Tennessee
Saddle Up!
1549 Old Hillsboro Road
Franklin, TN 37069-9136
Phone: (615) 794-1150
http://www.saddleupnashville.org/

Tennessee Council on Developmental Disabilities
404 James Robertson Parkway, Suite 130
Nashville, TN 37243-0228
Phone: (615) 532-6615
http://www.state.tn.us/cdd

Texas
PEN Project
1001 Main Street, Suite 804
Lubbock, TX 79401
Phone: (877) 762-1435
http://www.partnerstx.org/

Talking Book Program
Texas State Library and Archives Commission
P.O. Box 12927
Austin, TX 78711-2927
Phone: (800) 252-9605
http://www.texastalkingbooks.org/

Utah
Family Voices of Utah
Family-to-Family Health Information & Education
   Center
44 N. Medical Drive
P.O. Box 144650
Salt Lake City, UT 84114-4650
Phone: (800) 829-8200
http://www.familyvoices.org/

Utah Association for Intellectual Disabilities (UAID)
P. O. Box 25304
Salt Lake City, UT 84125
(801) 654-8449
http://www.arcutah.org/

Vermont
Vermont Association for the Blind and Visually
   Impaired
37 Elmwood Avenue
Burlington, VT 05401
Phone: (800) 639-5861
http://www.vabvi.org/

Vermont Coalition for Disability Rights
73 Main Street, Suite 402
Montpelier, VT 05602
Phone: (802) 223-6140
http://www.vcdr.org/

Virginia
Easter Seals Virginia
8003 Franklin Farms Drive, Suite 100
Richmond, VA 23229
Phone: (866) 874-4153
http://www.va.easterseals.com/

Kluge Children's Rehabilitation Center
P.O. Box 800673
Charlottesville, VA 22908
(434) 982-4925
http://hsc.virginia.edu/internet/dietetics/kluge.cfm

Washington
PAVE
Infant/Toddler Early Intervention Program
6316 S. 12th Street
Tacoma, WA 98465
Phone: (800) 572-7368
http://www.wapave.org/

Summit Assistance Dogs
7575 Chestnut Lane
Anacorte, WA 98221
Phone: (360) 293-5609
http://www.summitdogs.org/

West Virginia
Easter Seals West Virginia
1305 National Road
Wheeling, WV 26003-5780
Phone: (800) 677-1390
http://www.wv.easterseals.com/

West Virginia University Center for Excellence in
   Disabilities
959 Hartman Run Road
Morgantown, WV 26505
(304) 293-4692
http://www.cedwvu.org/

Wisconsin
University Center for Excellence in Developmental
   Disabilities
Waisman Center
University of Wisconsin
1500 Highland Avenue
Madison, WI 53705-2280
Phone: (608) 263-5776
http://www.waisman.wisc.edu/

Wisconsin Center for the Blind and Visually
   Impaired
1700 W. State Street
Janesville, WI 53546
Phone: (800) 832-9784 (in WI)
http://www.wcbvi.k12.wi.us/

Wyoming
VSA Arts of Wyoming
239 W. First Street
Casper, WY 82601
Phone: (307) 237-8618
http://vsawyo.org/

Wyoming Department of Health
Developmental Disabilities Division
6101 Yellowstone Road, Room 186E
Cheyenne, WY 82002
Telephone: (307) 777-7115
http://wdh.state.wy.us/ddd/index.html

Further Reading

Books

Gay, Kathlyn. *Volunteering: The Ultimate Teen Guide*. Lanham, MD: The Scarecrow Press, Inc., 2004.

Keating-Valasco, Joanna L. *A Is for Autism, F Is for Friend*. Shawnee Mission, KS: Autism Asperger Publishing Co., 2007.

Nixon, Shelley. *From Where I Sit: Making My Way With Cerebral Palsy*. New York: Scholastic, 1999.

Parkin, Jeff. *Mitchell's Story: Living with Cerebral Palsy*. Victoria, Canada: Trafford Publishing, 2003.

Works Consulted

Collier, J. Randall. *Onions in the Peanut Butter (My Problem Is Cerebral Palsy . . . What's Yours?)*. Kearney, NE: Morris Publishing, 1994.

Greenspan, Stanley I. *The Child with Special Needs*. Jackson, TN: Perseus Books Group, 1998.

James, Amy. *School Success for Children With Special Needs*. San Francisco: John Wiley & Sons, 2008.

Martin, Marilyn. *Helping Children with Nonverbal Learning Disabilities to Flourish*. London: Jessica Kingsley Publishers, 2007.

Nekola, Julie. *Helping Kids with Special Needs*. Minneapolis: Nekola Books, 2001.

Schwartz, Sue. *The New Language of Toys*. Bethesda, MD: Woodbine House, 2007.

Sicile-Kira, Chantal, and Temple Grandin. *Autism Spectrum Disorders: The Complete Guide to Understanding Autism, Asperger's Syndrome, Pervasive Developmental Disorder, and Other ASDs*. New York: The Berkley Publishing Group, 2004.

On the Internet

Center for Educational Networking
    http://www.cenmi.org

The Deal with Disability
    http://thedealwithdisability.blogspot.com/ Learn and Serve Challenge

Municipal Research and Services Center of Washington
    http://ww.mrsc.org

National Dissemination Center for Children with Disabilities
    http://www.nichcy.org

National Inclusion Project
    http://www.inclusionproject.org/

National Learn and Serve Challenge
    http://www.learnandservechallenge.org

National Service-Learning Partnership
    http://www.service-learningpartnership.org/

United Way
    http://www.liveunited.org/

Index

Karen Bush Gibson has written more than 30 educational books for children about different cultures, famous people, and events in history. Growing up with a younger brother who had developmental disabilities inspired her to study ways to help others in college. She graduated with an M.S.W. degree and worked as a social worker for twelve years. Her favorite time as a social worker was working with children in Oklahoma with developmental disabilities.